IMAGES
of England

AROUND DORKING AND BOX HILL

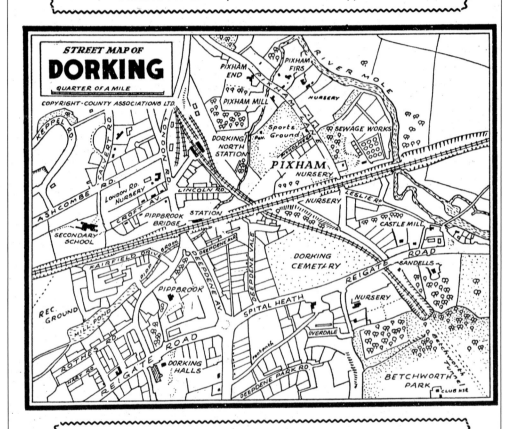

A street map of Dorking in 1938, showing the eastern end of the town and the new junction of the A24 and A25. The two railway lines run from east to west and north to south. The cemetery is five minutes' walk from the town centre. Pippbrook House, now Dorking library, sits in its own gardens on Reigate Road.

IMAGES
of England

AROUND
DORKING AND
BOX HILL

Compiled by
June M. Spong

TEMPUS

First published 1999
Copyright © June M. Spong, 1999

Tempus Publishing Limited
The Mill, Brimscombe Port,
Stroud, Gloucestershire, GL5 2QG

ISBN 0 7524 1152 7

Typesetting and origination by
Tempus Publishing Limited
Printed in Great Britain by
Midway Clark Printing, Wiltshire

This book is dedicated to my parents, Dorothy May (Muscato) Knowles 1909 - 1998 and George Henry Knowles 1908 - 1976, who are now together at rest.

Dorking's Coat of Arms. This represents the ancient Manor of Dorking with the gold and blue cheques of the Warrennes; the arms are considered the oldest truly heraldic coat of arms in England. The first Earl of Warrenne and Surrey received the manor with his bride, the daughter of William I. From them it descended down to the FitzAlans of Arundel, who bore a gold lion on red. Above the shield is the closed helm proper to civic arms, with its decorative cloak or mantle in the main colours of gold and blue, the traditional Surrey liveries. The helm is surmounted by a mural or walled crown of white. Out of the crown is a mound representing the heights of Box Hill and standing upon it is a Dorking Cock. The motto *Virtute et Vigiliantia* means 'By Courage and Vigilance'.

Contents

An aerial view of Dorking in 1933. This date can be accurately established, as the construction of the houses in Fairfield Drive began that year. The ancillary road has been marked out, with the two traffic islands clearly visible. The first of the larger houses can be seen under construction by the tip of St Martin's spire. The view clearly shows the High Street going east and South Street snaking west. At the bottom right-hand corner is the spire of the Wesleyan church. The United Reformed church stands proud to the left. Cotmandene and the sand pits are just below Box Hill, while Pixham lies to the left of the picture at the bottom of the hill. It is interesting to note how many trees there are in and around the town.

Acknowledgements

This book has been produced with the help and encouragement of my husband George. Many of the photographs produced are from my varied collection of postcards. We would also like to thank Mr Alan Woodcock and Mr David Fuller, both long established members of Dorking's community, and Mr James Coughlan, a friend and fellow postcard collector. Without their help and the loan of their pictures this book would not have been possible. Also, I am grateful for the help of Mr John Janaway and the Surrey Archives from which I was able to reproduce a selection of rural photographs. Thanks also are due to Dorking Library for the use of a selection from the varied collection housed in their local history cabinet.

I must thank Mr Janaway, once again, for his always encouraging support.

Introduction

Dorking is an ancient market town in the county of Surrey. It stands in the valley of the River Mole, just below the North Downs. It is twenty-nine miles south west of London. Dorking is the centre of a scenic area comprising Box Hill, Leith Hill and Ranmore. One of its commons, Cotmandene, is of special interest in the cricket world: Walter Caffyn played cricket on 'the Dene', which was as well known as the Oval 100 years ago.

There are four railway stations that serve Dorking and Box Hill: three are within ten minutes' walk from the town centre: Dorking, the main station (once called Dorking North), Deepdene (first known as Boxhill) and Dorking West (first called Dorking Town). The fourth is Box Hill and Mickleham, which lies in the Dorking Gap and is adjacent to Box Hill and the Burford Bridge Hotel. There are two main railway lines which serve the community. The east to west runs from Tunbridge Wells to Reading via Guildford, and the north to south runs from London to Horsham.

Dorking has a number of claims to fame. It is noted for a breed of chicken which takes its name from the town where it was extensively bred. The chief and most prominent building is St Martin's church, rebuilt in the late nineteenth century. The former King's Head pub in North Street is said to have been the inspiration for the Marquis of Granby pub featured in Charles Dickens' *Pickwick Papers*. In the vicinity is some of the finest scenery in Surrey, including Box Hill, Leith Hill, Betchworth, Abinger, Friday Street, Wotton and Ranmore.

Lime burning was one of the area's main industries. The lime pits prospered in the early nineteenth century and the scars on the Downs can be seen in many places. The trade prospered after the railways came to the town, by which fine lime was transported to London, and continued until the end of the Second World War. Dorking also had a thriving iron foundry and its horseshoes were the best in the county. There were many watermills in the area. Dorking had its own gas and light company, and the first waterworks were founded in 1735.

Near to Box Hill stood two fine mansions, Pippbrook and Deepdene. One of these, the grand mansion of Deepdene House and its vast grounds, has now gone. It was once the home of the Hope family who owned the Hope Diamond, later a hotel.

Many famous and infamous people are synonymous with Dorking. George Meredith, the favourite poet of Queen Victoria, lived 'on the hill', as did John Logie Baird, the inventor of television. John Keats visited it, and so too did Jane Austen, Celia Fiennes, Queen Victoria, Daniel Defoe, Robert Louis Stevenson and Samuel Pepys. Many came to stay, such as Fanny Burney, Leslie Howard, Abraham Hulk, Dr Marie Stopes, Ralph Vaughan Williams, Sir Arthur Cotton, Sir Thomas Cubitt and Richard Brinsley Sheridan. Others left, including William Mullins, Walter Dendy Sadler, Sir Laurence Olivier and Walter Caffyn, who took the game of cricket to Australia.

Box Hill lies just north of Dorking. It has one of the natural sights of Surrey, a view from the summit which 'no Englishman can see without a thrill of pride'. There is an ancient ford over the River Mole, so named because it disappears beneath the ground into the chalk subterranean clefts, to reappear again near Leatherhead. The ford by the Burford is presumed to have been a natural crossing for the pilgrims making their way from Canterbury to Winchester over the North Downs.

Westhumble, with its ruined chapel, lies to the west of the A24; the only road leads to Polesden Lacy. The playwright Richard Brinsley Sheridan had a house nearby, built on land owned by his family. The building, with its terrace 300 yards long, is now in the keeping of the National Trust. King George VI and his bride, Elizabeth Bowes Lyon, spent their honeymoon here with Mrs Greville. Edward VII and George V were also frequent visitors. Polesden Lacy is now the office of the National Trust's Southern Region. During the summer months many visitors are attracted to the performances that are arranged there.

Mickleham nestles at the foot of the hill. It was the home of Fanny Burney who later became Madame Frances d'Arblay. Fanny married her French Count in the church of St Michael, which is mentioned in the *Domesday Book* and certainly existed before the Norman Conquest.

Box Hill overlooks Ranmore Common and Leith Hill, where the famous tower sits. Known 'as the crown of Surrey', the folly attracts many thousands of walkers. This is also part of the many acres held by the National Trust. The top of the tower is 1,029 feet above sea level. It stands not only at the highest place in Surrey, but also in a great area of England. Nothing as high comes between it and the coast to south or east, and the nearest rival height to the west is 100 miles away in the Mendip Hills. Below is the vast patchwork of the Weald, and beyond are the South Downs, with Chanctonbury Ring and a glimpse of the sea through Shoreham Gap.

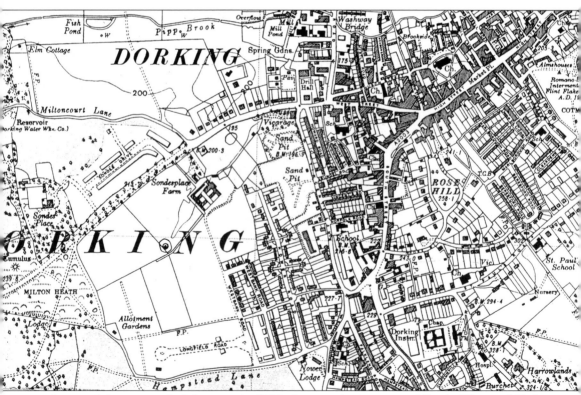

A map of the west end of the town in 1938, showing the junction of South, West and High Streets.

One
Old Dorking

The Dorking Fowl is a breed of chicken deriving its name from the town where it was, at one time, extensively bred and fattened. A peculiar characteristic of the breed is that it possesses a fifth toe. Compact, plump in build, and broad in the breast, it carries more meat in proportion to the size of its bones than any other fowl; in quality and flavour its flesh is excellent. As a layer, the hen compares favourably with any other birds of its size and weight. It excels both as a sitter and mother. There are three main varieties; these are the Red, Silver Grey and Dark Dorkings. The earliest reference to the Dorking breeds appear in *The Poultry Review* in December 1873. There is speculation that the Romans brought the breed to England. Queen Victoria's diners were known to have feasted on the Dorking Fowl.

The sight of a chained bear in Dorking High Street is long gone, thank goodness. This cruel sport was common from the seventeenth to the late nineteenth centuries and prior to the Second World War was still a common sight in Europe. This view dates from around 1880. The travelling gipsies owned and kept tame bears which they showed at fairs and markets. In his book *Between the Woods and Water* Patrick Leigh Fermour recounts how he stumbled across a sleeping bear whilst staying at a gipsy encampment in Bosnia in 1937.

Above: A cottage in Dorking churchyard from a sketch by R.H. Major, *c.* 1750. *Below*: A view of old Dorking by an unknown artist, *c.* 1750. From *Recollections of Old Dorking* by Charles Rose, April 1878: 'The Dorking of fifty years ago was different in many aspects from Dorking today.... Let us first, however, get a glimpse of the old town by an imaginary walk through its streets. We enter the place by London Road, say on a summer's morning half a century ago. Although yet early, the mill by the roadside is already at work, and the forge of the blacksmith's shop at Reigate Road corner is in full blast. We pass along by the southern entrance of the neighbouring nursery grounds.... The chestnut trees hard by, the broad green meadow, the mill-pond, and the distant hill are each of them objects of beauty. On the left hand is an antiquated-looking brick mansion, owned and occupied by a noble lady.... It is only a little after six, yet many of the shops are ready to open, for the trading inhabitants of a half century ago were early risers.... Places of worship were few; old, or as it may be called, ancient St Martin's church, was then the sole Episcopalian church.'

Charles Huffam Dickens (1812-1870), the English novelist, was born in Portsea, the son of a clerk in the Navy Office. Dickens' childhood was spent at Chatham, with its fortified barracks, arsenal, artillery park and military school and institute. His early life must have been filled with great adventure. 'The childhood of Dickens, in its general outlines, may be studied in the early chapters of *David Copperfield,* also in his portrait of young Pip in *Great Expectations.* He must have been the most observant of children, wise beyond his years.' Dickens is reputed to have penned *Pickwick Papers* whilst on one of his many visits to Dorking. The first monthly number of *Pickwick Papers* appeared on 31 March 1836 and it was an unparalleled success. He is said to have modelled the Marquis of Granby public house on the White Horse Hotel, below.

This is most likely the scene that Charles Dickens would have seen on one of his many visits to Dorking. The wide High Street was a dirt road where markets traded every week. Charles also frequented the Old King's Head in North Street.

The White Horse has little changed over the last two centuries. A glass of ale can still be supped in the lounge by a roaring fire in winter. The friendly staff are willing to serve your every need. The oak beams and the curved staircase stand as they did two centuries ago. To sit in the cobblestone courtyard on a sunny day is a pleasant way of spending an hour or two.

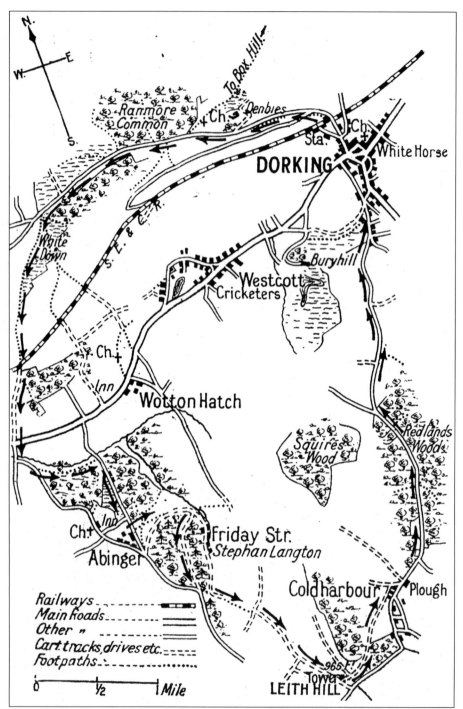

From *The Ramblers' Guide to Dorking and Environs*, No. 1: 'It would be difficult to find in England a finer day's walk than this one over the North Downs, across the valley below, up the slope of Leith Hill, the highest point in south-east England, and thence back through the woods to Dorking.... This affords fine views over the valley. Still hold to the road until the Common is reached. There is a wonderful two miles of walking until the Common's boundary is reached.'

14

The White Horse is the best known inn in Dorking because of its location and because it is the oldest known of the many inns. It enhances one of the most pleasant-looking town centres in the area. It stands on the old Stane Street and was known as a resting place for many of the early travellers – perhaps for at least a thousand years. The earliest evidence of a building on this site dates from 1278. It is thought that some of the earlier parts of the building can still be found under the foundations of the present inn. The frontage leading onto the High Street dates from the turn of the eighteenth century. Some parts underneath the main structure can be dated to the fifteenth and sixteenth centuries. The White Horse became an inn in 1750 and since has served the town as a coaching inn.

Dorking was a major market town and cattle came on the hoof from as far away as Portsmouth, through Guildford, over the Downs and through to Sevenoaks, and then on to the slaughter yards of London such as Aldgate, Smithfield, Highgate and Holloway. The salted meat then went on to Chatham and Tilbury to feed the troops. The sights and sounds, hustle and bustle and smells of the cattle markets of earlier centuries cannot compare with the sound of the traffic today. London and its soldiers had to be fed, and so did the local community. Droving started in the Neolithic period when tribes were in continuous search for fresh grazing pastures; this was some 6,000 years ago. Dorking stands on one of the ancient trackways, Stane Street, which later became one of the four 'Royal Roads'.

Apart from beef cattle, calves, sheep, lambs, goats and pigs, there was other livestock that passed through the market place for general consumption. There could also be seen venison and pheasant that was destined for the tables of the great houses. There was also a regular fowl market of geese, duck, chickens, woodcock and wood pigeons. The breeds of chicken sold here were probably the Light Sussex and the Dorking. Eggs were another commodity, along with rabbit and hare. These were shot or snared by the gamekeepers and their labourers. Rabbit was generally consumed by the working classes. Goats were farmed in great numbers. They are a fast-growing animal and reach maturity within six months. The female can start producing milk at six months old without gestation, and at eleven months can give birth to two or three young – multiple births are common for goats.

On market days, hair-cutting was performed on a three-legged stool. The market was held in the High Street, just outside the White Horse. The markets moved to the new Market Place in 1926. The Market Place was closed in the early 1960s and is now St Martin's Walk. There is still a shoppers' market held each Friday in the St Martin's Walk car park.

The south end of the High Street at the junction of North, West and South Streets. There were once seven alehouses and inns at this part of the town: the Old King's Head, the Queen's Arms and the Gun in North Street, the Chequers, the Wheatsheaf and the Bull's Head in the High Street, and the White Lion on the corner of South Street. Chequers Yard is to the extreme right. It must be a weekday as there are many carts making deliveries. In the foreground is the baker's van, to the left is the dilapidated entrance to the post office which eventually fell down.

Mill Lane runs from the High Street down a very steep slope to the Mill Pond. At the bottom of the lane is the Recreation Ground, Dorking Football Club and the Malthouse public house. The name was originally the Rising Sun; it is relatively new compared to many other public houses in Dorking. At the turn of the century Mill Lane housed Mr Blaker's tanyard, Boxell's brewery and small tenement houses. Woolworths now stands to the right, and the new St Martin's Walk is to the left.

A view from the post office towards the southern end of the High Street, in the 1930s. The expansion of the White Horse Hotel is quite visible. The large building at the extreme left was occupied by the South Eastern Gas Board show rooms. It is now occupied by Fuller's wholesale wine company.

The Market House Inn and the Three Tuns 'Family & Commercial Hotel', c. 1900. Both face the Red Lion Hotel in the centre of the High Street. There seems to be little traffic and few pedestrians – it could possibly be on a Sunday, as both the gentleman and the child seem to be in their Sunday best.

An aerial view of the High Street, c. 1935. The fourteenth-century White Horse Hotel with its splendid exposed timber frame stands on the east side. In the foreground is the Market Place with the Three Tuns public house on the west side of the street. The Cotmandene is in the background, standing high above the town with Deepdene House just visible in the mist. The Market Place was used as a car park for many years when the cattle market was no longer held in Dorking. The Red Lion Hotel is to the extreme right of the photograph; part of it has a timber-framed frontage.

Ram Alley, later named Dene Street, in 1904, with the Ram Inn on the left. The proprietor in 1891 was Samuel Arnold. The shop with the awning is Fuller's the butchers.

Looking up Dene Street with the White Hart on the left. The landlord in 1891 was Benjamin Rose. This has changed little over the last century. The prominent chimneys belong to the Jolly Butchers, whose landlord in 1891 was Mr Rish. There also stood another alehouse in Dene Street, the Bricklayers Arms, whose landlord in 1891 was Mrs M.A. Page. The houses made way for council flats in the late 1950s. Cotmandene is approached by a short hill to the left. Dene Street leads to Chart Lane and the Holmwoods.

Dene Street again, now looking towards the High Street, *c.* 1900. The bollards from Dorking's iron foundry went many years ago. The horse and cart are coming from Cotmandene down Heath Hill.

The High Street looking north, *c.* 1880. The town is well established now with many shops. The house just beyond the large oak tree is Rosenburge; it was owned by the Fuller family who had properties in South Street and High Street. Its name was changed to Rosefields during the First World War. The property was demolished in the early 1950s. The Ram Inn stands on the corner of Dene Street to the extreme right.

The Surrey Yeoman, originally called the Royal Oak, is believed to be over 400 years old and stood at the entrance of the town. According to a list held in the Local Record Office dated 1750 it was 'frequented by a low class of people and suspected people'. It was the first meeting place of the Royal Order of Buffaloes (Oddfellows). The Oddfellows' Hall was built a few doors down. There is reputed to be a right of way through the old inn from the High Street to Cotmandene.

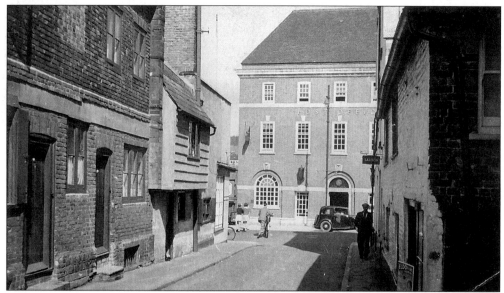

Dene Street, looking towards the post office building. The first post office was opposite the Wheatsheaf Inn, then on the corner of North Street in front of the Old King's Head. In *Recollections of Old Dorking* Charles Rose recorded that the mail-coach stopped at the post office opposite the Wheatsheaf Inn. In 1828, Postman Beadle charged 6d for out-of-town letters. A 6d charge was made on letters from London, and was paid on delivery on a once-a-day basis. There was a thrice-a-day delivery service of the one-penny mail. The post office moved into the Council Chambers in South Street before it moved into its new premises on the corner of Ansell Road in 1936.

The Ram Inn in the High Street, in a photograph by Mr Styles from 1952. The Ram was pulled down in 1957 to make way for modern shops. It was outside the Ram where, on a Sunday morning, the troops of the Dorking Yeomanry Cavalry breakfasted before their journey to London to escort Sir Francis Burdett MP (1770-1844) to the Tower of London, after his speech in the House of Lords on the Reform Act. Burdett had made himself unpopular by insisting that flogging be stopped in prisons, and that Habeas Corpus and freedom of speech be suspended. It was said that, fearful of the consequences, the troops made their wills. Thomas Hart practised as a solicitor and Clerk of the Magistrates in a lane facing the Ram in the early nineteenth century. His son, John Hart, continued there. The solicitors, Hart, Scales & Hodges practise in virtually the same place. The Treasure Chest, to the right of the inn, was probably the first antique shop in Dorking.

Cheesman & Bromley

(R. J. Cheesman)

DORKING

10 & 12 HIGH STREET

for

Men's and Boys' Ready-to-wear Clothing of all kinds
Underwear in all the leading makes
Shirts in large variety
Overalls and Mechanics' Clothing of all descriptions
Hats, Caps, Gloves, Raincoats, Macs, etc.

Specialists in Tailoring Made to Measure

Suits, Overcoats, Breeches, Costumes, etc.
at competitive prices

An advertisement for Cheesman and Bromley, men's outfitters.

Chequers Yard, between the 'shippers' and the camera shop, c. 1910. The shops at this end of the town have changed little in their general appearance. The iron rails and bollards are still in place. The pavement is high and there are cellars leading from each of the shops under the road. The building with the clock was the old candle factory. Above the façade is the inscription 'Let there be light'. Cheesman & Bromley was just a few doors from Chequers Yard. Cheesman was a common name in the Dorking area at this time.

Woodcock's the chemist in 1934. It has been a chemist's shop since before the turn of the century. The name over the first shop was Doubleday's, then it became Dixon's in 1908. On market days, a travelling dentist used to extract teeth on the high pavement in front of the shop. Mr Alan Woodcock bought the business in 1934 and lived over the shop with his family for nineteen years. The business was sold in 1995. The Woodcocks still have an interest in the business. Below is the interior of the shop – little has changed over the last 100 years. The carboys can still be seen, the glass jars still adorn the window, and the array of jars containing 'strange substances' still adorn the high shelves. It has only changed slightly in the past two years.

The Old Dutch House, seen here in a nineteenth-century drawing and a 1960s photograph by Mr Alan Woodcock. It was converted into three houses after its sale in 1820 and the frontage was added somewhat later. It was afterwards converted into three shops – a chemist, a fishmongers and a hardware shop. Later, the White Horse added the shop to the left to its existing building. The old chimneys are still visible at the rear of the building. The original oak beams and rafters have recently been dated to 1558 from a date in Roman numerals carved by the carpenter.

The Red Lion Hotel, *c.* 1880. Before its demise, this building saw many events and roles. It was the magistrates' house, a smugglers' retreat and from the steps came the election results. It has seen riots, demonstrations and various social activities and became a popular meeting place. There was an alehouse on the ground floor called The Grapes and even a dentist's surgery in the basement.

The Red Lion building in the early 1960s. The entrance to the Milk Bar is visible to the left. That part of the building now displays a timber-framed frontage. The Milk Bar flourished until the building was demolished. The old building also housed Barclays Bank for a short time while the bank's new premises were rebuilt across the road. The Red Lion Hotel closed for business in 1964. The building was in very bad repair and was demolished in the same year to make way for a parade of new shops.

The Sun Inn is being demolished to make way for Curry's electrical shop and a shoe shop. The International Stores later made way for the Etam fashion shop. The date on the billboard is 1970. (Photograph by Mr Alan Woodcock)

The High Street just outside the White Horse Hotel, 1945. Woolworths is called 'the 3d and 6d stores'. On the corner of Mill Lane and the High Street stands Usherwood's the photographers, next is Walker's coach builders and garage. The post office is the tallest building to the east. (Photograph by Mr Alan Woodcock)

The High Street again. The shops facing the White Horse Hotel are: Robert Hicks, Pearks the grocers and Hart, Scales and Hodges the solicitors. John Dendy Sadler had his solicitors' offices here in the 1851 and 1861 censuses. His son, Walter Dendy Sadler (1854-1923), was born in Dorking. He became a notable artist of fishing scenes. He liked to fish, and painted to earn money to do so. Walter lived for most of his life in a house by the River Ouse in St Ives, near Huntingdon. In his will he bequeaths 'nothing to my eldest son, as he has had it all before'.

Looking east down the High Street in around 1952, with the Red Lion Hotel decked with bunting. The sign to the public bar of the Grapes is clearly visible. Clifford's is the shop on the left selling Calor gas. It later became a branch of W.H. Smith. There is a good view of Box Hill in the background.

The Three Tuns Inn, *c*. 1890. This was originally the corn market where merchants 'pitched for grain'. At one time there was a large seat or settle of considerable length for public use. It was on this site that the local rat-catcher would cry 'Death to the rats' to encourage trade.

The later site of the Three Tuns, at the entrance of the new market place. The picture dates from around 1940 as the Parkway estate is clearly visible behind the market entrance. Parkway was built in the mid to late 1930s by Mr A.F. Davis, a speculative builder from London.

The Three Tuns
being demolished to
make way for the
Tesco supermarket
in 1973. The market
place became a car
park and the town
lost some of its
character. The
supermarket ceased
to trade in the late
eighties and the new
St Martin's Walk,
with a number of
smaller shops, took
its place.

The south end of the High Street, *c.* 1900. H.C. Kingham & Co. is the shop displaying all its wares. It was a wholesale grocers, wine and spirit merchants. They established themselves in the town in 1893. As well as their shop at 20-28 High Street, they had their warehouse in Station Road, which is at the southern end of West Street. They had fourteen branches in all in Kent, Surrey and Sussex. Kingham's sold out to Cullen's in 1969. W.H. Smith is at No. 29.

A little way further up the High Street at the turn of the twentieth century. F.W. Lloyd and the sign of the Wheatsheaf Inn are clearly visible. There was another public house in the High Street called the Black Horse. The carriage could well belong to the Forman family of Pippbrook House or perhaps the Hopes of Deepdene.

Looking south towards the junction of South, West and North Streets. The London Book Company is on the extreme right and the *Dorking Advertiser* resides next door. The gas street lights have been erected and in 1894 there were 200 lamps lighting the town. The camera shop on the left is displaying its 'Kodak' sign.

Looking west along the High Street, *c.* 1890. There is a veterinary practice and forge with a white picket fence around it. Next to the forge is Rosenburge (later known as Rosefields) owned by the Fuller family. They also owned a butchers shop at the junction of Dene Street. The sign of the Surrey Yeoman is plainly visible and the Ram is in the distance.

The High Street facing north around the turn of the twentieth century. The Edmonds Brothers' 'Art Dress Warehouse' occupies three large premises. G. Inglefield Ltd later opened it as a general haberdashery. They thrived until its closure in 1930. Mr Will Robins, who had become manager of the haberdashers and milliners, then opened a furniture store. Mr Robins brought up his family, three sons and a daughter over the shop. Robins continued to trade until its closure in December 1997.

Looking back along the south end of the High Street and its parade of shops on a Sunday morning in 1953.

In this 1960 view, the shops have changed slightly with the advent of more modern requirements. Two shoe shops sit side by side: Bata Shoes and John Farmer.

By 1971 Bata Shoes has been replaced by Freeman, Hardy & Willis and one of the first travel agencies in the town is trading. Next to Bales Travel is an opticians, and Derek Gardner the photographer has a very appropriate shop sign.

Old St Martin's church. The older church with its square tower dominated this site. This picture was taken before the present-day church was started in 1868. The houses are in Church Street, known then as Back Lane. At this time, there were few places of worship in Dorking. Old St Martin's church was the only Episcopalian church. It was attended by parishioners from the Holmwoods, Coldharbour and Westcott. The nearest church to the west was Wotton, on the hill just past Westcott. There is an oil painting of Old St Martin's by John Beckett, who was a resident of Dorking.

Two
The New Churches

The interior of the present-day St Martin's in 1902. It is a large and handsome building and is well furnished. St Martin's boasts two fine stained glass windows depicting the coats of arms of the Burt and Forman families. Elizabeth and Thomas Forman took a very active part in Dorking life; they were also noted for the founding of the new church.

St Martin's was rebuilt twice during the second half of the nineteenth century. The present day church was constructed between 1869 and 1877 and the foundation stone of the new tower was laid in 1873. The bells were hung in 1877 but had to be removed in March 1998 to allow repair work to be carried out on the bell tower. New bells to ring in the new millennium were hung in April 1998 and first pealed out on 19 May.

Old St Martin's church dominated the skyline. This view was possibly painted from Leith Hill or Coldharbour. There was a Roman encampment near Stane Street which is supposed to run parallel to the High Street.

The new church at the turn of the century, seen from Church Street. The houses have changed little in the past ninety years. The house on the left nearest to the tower was replaced in 1933 by Church Court. It was built by E.H. Cummings & Co. for Dorking Urban District Council. The bricks were made locally by the Dorking Brick Company Ltd.

Church Passage. The houses have been replaced by shops and offices. The Revd Henry Joyce, born in 1817 and educated at Charterhouse and Oxford, was ordained in 1842. He became curate at Dorking whilst his father held the living. William then succeeded his father in 1850. For a period of thirty-three years the parish of St Martin was served by the same family. William's brother, the Revd John Wayland Joyce, had been curate to his father from 1838 to 1843, and later his nephew, the Revd James Barclay Joyce, son of John Wayland Joyce, also served as curate from 1875 to 1876.

St Martin's on a bright winter's day in 1963 from one of the offices at the back of the High Street. The picture was taken by Mr Alan Woodcock, a keen photographer as well as the town's chemist.

St Paul's Church, Dorking.

St Paul's church in St Paul's Road, 1907. To fulfil the demand of the growing population of Dorking, the building of a second Anglican church was undertaken. St Paul's church was completed in 1857, and was designed by Benjamin Ferrey. Ferrey also designed the rectory next door. It sits in a quiet suburb to the south of the town, only a short walk from Cotmandene.

St Joseph's Catholic church was erected 1895 in Falkland Grove, off of Coldharbour Lane. The design was by Frederick Arthur Walters on a site donated by the Duke of Norfolk, who also gave a substantial donation to the cost of the building of the church. The church is a short distance from The Nower, another parkland area of Dorking.

Dismantling the Wesleyan church in South Street in the late 1960s. The church housed a youth club in the cellars during the 1950s but was later demolished to make way for shops. John Wesley visited Dorking in January 1764. This was first of many visits over the next twenty-two years. Meetings were first held in the Red Lion Hotel until an established meeting house was secured in Church Street. This meeting house still stands in the car park of the King's Arms. (Photograph by Mr Alan Woodcock)

St Martin's church dominating the skyline. The warren of small houses in this area were demolished to provide a substantial car park for the inner town. The back entrance of Sainsbury's and Robert Dyas are to the left. Dorking Deep Freeze ceased to trade in the early 1980s.

The church of St Barnabas sits 700ft above Dorking on Ranmore Common. It was designed by Sir Gilbert Scott in 1859 as the estate church for George Cubitt, the first Lord Ashcombe. In the churchyard lies the founder of the church and the Denbies Estate. It has a noble chapel with a portrait of Lord Ashcombe who built the church; there are beautiful frescoes in memory of his three grandsons, Henry, Alick and William Cubitt, who lost their lives in the First World War. Lord Ashcombe's father, Thomas Cubitt, built up the family fortune: beginning life as a carpenter in 1788, by the time of Waterloo (1815) he was able to build the London Institution in Finsbury Circus.

Three
The Mills

Westcott Mill, *c*. 1880. There were three watermills operating in Dorking in the eighteenth century. The Rookery was also fed by the Pipprook which ran through the grounds of Milton Court. The owner of Westcott mill at the end of the nineteenth century was James Bravery. Westcott is one of the many parishes attached to Dorking.

A view of the River Mole at the back of Castle Mill dated 7 August 1887.

Castle Mill, *c.* 1890. The mill was fed by the River Mole. One of its owners was George Dewdney. It was one of the last to continue as a working mill, ceasing to operate in 1952.

The Pippbrook Mill Stream, *c.* 1870. The willow trees are still a prominent feature around the Mill Pond, which fed Pippbrook Watermill. The course of the stream was later changed and its volume reduced to make a more picturesque setting for the town.

Pippbrook Mill, sometimes known as Patching Mill because of its connections with the Patching family who owned it at one time. It is situated in London Road and started its working life in 1649; this date is engraved on the entrance door to the mill. The mill ceased to operate in 1932. The mill suffered a fire while being used as a warehouse for mattresses. Under instructions of the local council at the time, it was rebuilt to its original design. It is now the offices of a publishing company.

Willow Walk, looking west towards Mill Lane and St Martin's church. The Mill Pond is on the right. Little has changed during the last ninety years since this photograph was taken, except that there were once nut trees and mulberry trees lining the other side of the Pippbrook. There were also workshops and a large greenhouse.

Willow Walk looking east towards the Pippbrook Mill again. The Mill Pond teems with wildlife all year round. There are numerous ducks of varied size and colour. Swans now inhabit the pond again after a short break in the late eighties. A flock of black-headed gulls can be seen all year round, and the occasional flock of Canada geese visits whilst migrating south.

MILL POND, DORKING 12

Meadowbank and the Mill Pond, looking towards Pippbrook Mill and Box Hill. Meadowbank and its twenty-nine acres of grounds were bought by Dorking Urban District Council in 1926. The intention was to build a council estate of over 150 houses, but the scheme proved too costly for the council. It was later bought by Mr Maurice Chance, a property developer. He started building the houses in Fairfield Drive but was unable to complete his ambition. The pond is fed by the Pippbrook which runs between the Malthouse public house and the Dorking Football Club.

Four
South and West Dorking

North Street, looking from the High Street, 1902. According to the 1891 census, the proprietor of the Old King's Head was Caleb Browning. The Gun Inn is on the opposite side of the street. The buildings are now occupied by boutiques, a travel agency, accountants' offices and a building society.

North Street in 1967, looking towards the High Street. The photographer is standing at the junction of Church Street, with the Waterworks just a few yards behind him.

Fielder's Drapers and Tailors, No. 1 High Street, *c.* 1834. The proprietor in 1891 was Robert W. Fielder. His son Frank was seventeen and was a pupil to a photographer. He produced fine watercolour paintings of the local area. The building is presently occupied by Millets. The name of Fielder can still be seen embossed in the brickwork above the shop.

South Street at the junction with the High Street, *c.* 1905. The Bull's Head inn is on the extreme right of the picture. The White Lion inn is the last building on the left hand side of the street. The new spire of St Martin's dominates the town.

54

In the 1850s the scene looks totally different. The White Lion is a prominent feature. The Bulls Head looks bigger, Fielder's is just visible beyond. The Queens Arms is still standing on the corner of North Street and the High Street. The bow-fronted house looks in need of repair.

South Street, Dorking

Looking back again to the High Street. The photographer would have been standing in front of the hardware shop. The dismal building on the left seems to be an employment exchange. The shop between it and the White Lion is virtually unchanged today. On the right is a better view of the Bulls Head, and the marble shop front of Chitty's the butcher can be seen quite clearly.

Looking south along South Street, *c.* 1880. On the corner is a hardware shop; it must be approaching 5 November, as a sign advertises fireworks. The next shop is a gents' hairdressers and next to that is Fuller's first bicycle shop. The shop on the right is displaying its shoes. The notice says 'American Overshoes 2d'. These buildings on the left were demolished in 1920.

A hundred yards further south, with the Spotted Dog public house on the extreme left, *c.* 1880. It looks much the same today with its bow windows. Rowe's the stationers are still there, but the shops and houses on the right were demolished in 1920 to make way for the bandstand and War Memorial.

The shops and houses in South Street in the 1880s, including Stanford's shop. Jack Stanford was the town crier.

The houses and shops in South Street undergoing demolition, *c.* 1920. They were situated in front of Butter Hill. Note the workman by the ladder on the top of the high building.

A row of shops housing the post office and council chamber, a garage and Crypto Motor Cycles. Next to that is a shop selling work clothes – there is a manikin outside displaying overalls. The new buildings that exist today were built in the early 1970s and are occupied by Waterstones and Waitrose.

Halfway along South Street, *c.* 1912. The only house of those to the right of the picture still standing is the cottage on the extreme right. The remaining buildings made way for first the Co-operative Society and then a parade of new shops in the early 1970s. The post office and council chambers are on the corner of Junction Road. The shops and cottages on the right are virtually the same.

The Arch at Rose Hill, *c.* 1870. Rose Hill was a park with only a single house in 1828. There were gardens and allotments behind the High Street shops. There is a hive of sandstone caves under South Street and the High Street. This entrance leads to the Rose Hill estate which was built between 1838 and 1860. It is now the exit from Sainsbury's car park.

The Stoneroof Café. This was the home of Colour Sergeant Frank Bourne who took part in the Battle of Rorke's Drift in South Africa in 1879. He was born on 27 April 1855. For his bravery he was awarded the DCM and an annuity of £10. He later went to India with the regiment, serving in the Burma campaign of 1886. He retired from the army in 1909 but joined again at the beginning of the First World War. He was awarded the OBE for his services after serving forty-six years in the regiment. Active and upright to the end, he died aged 90. In the 1964 film *Zulu*, Nigel Green played Sgt Bourne.

French's Tea Garden, *c.* 1910. Mr French is standing in front of his establishment with his assistants. The tearooms were just a few yards from Junction Road. The Stoneroof Café is next door. In the 1960s it was a nursery school, but has now reverted to a café and gymnasium.

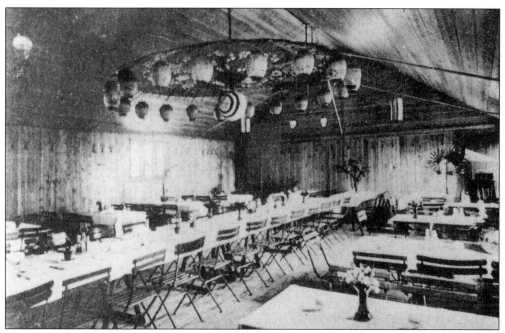

The interior of French's Tea Rooms. It could accommodate quite a large number of clients. It possibly specialized in cycle and touring clubs. South Street was then the main A24 road from London to Horsham and Worthing and the tearooms would have made a convenient half-way stop.

The garden area at the back of the tearooms. The staff look as though they are posing for advertising purposes.

The Brooms Dairy in South Street, two doors north of the Spotted Dog public house, 1940. Fuller's bicycle shop is next door. The Old Dairy closed its doors in 1939. It used to have a golden cow and calf mounted on a marble slab in the window. The shop was later owned by Mr Alan Woodcock. It was renovated and remodelled as his second chemist's shop. It is now Frith's Chemist. In 1935 there were eight chemists in Dorking, including Boots the Chemist. (Photograph by Mr Alan Woodcock)

The Spotted Dog public house, No. 67 South Street, in the 1920s. Rowe's shop has now become a printers and stationers.

Looking north down South Street towards the War Memorial, *c.* 1950. The bandstand stands out in front of the Bull's Head, now half tiled.

Looking south along South Street, with the bandstand on the left, *c.* 1930. The inscription on the bandstand reads: 'To the memory of his fellow townsmen who suffered and died for their country (1914-1918) and in gratitude for victory. This bandstand is dedicated by Charles Edmond Hall.' The bandstand was removed in the early 1970s and disappeared without trace.

An aerial view of South Street showing the 'Rotunda' (the round building) with Rose Hill House behind it. Butter Hill and the bandstand are clearly visible. The white building in the foreground is the Gun public house, and opposite is The Old King's Head which was frequented by Charles Dickens. Both pubs have gone now.

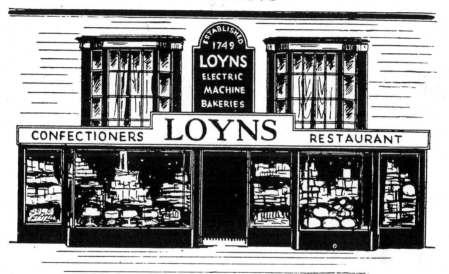
There used to be many teashops in Dorking. Lyon's was the largest, standing at the junction of South, North, West and High Streets. It survived for around 220 years, providing refreshment to the many visitors who visited this thriving market town. At one point there were thirty-six public houses, hotels and ale-houses and eight or ten teashops and confectioners.

A 1960s view near the Bull Ring, where bulls used to be baited. The bakery and confectioners was established in 1779. As far as is known, the ovens are still under this part of the High Street. This prominent building stands on Pump Corner. The pump is quite visible between Loyns and Margaretta Mills. The town pump was once a major source of water before the waterworks were established; this was the centre of the town.

The corner of West Street and the High Street. The picture must have been taken in the early 1950s as the concrete anti-tank reinnforcements are still in the High Street. Margaretta Mills was an established milliners. The post office stood on the corner of North Street before it moved to South Street.

West Street Forge at the junction of Westcott Road, Station Road and West Street, looking towards Westcott, 1902. Charles Rose writes in *Recollections of Old Dorking* (1878): 'We see here, on the left hand, the old barn where in autumn the produce of the 'Pupper', or 'Popper', (after it ceased to be a furze field) was gleaned, and where in winter the stroke of the thresher's flail resounded'.

West Street in 1902, looking in the opposite direction towards the town. The building on the extreme left is virtually unchanged. The first building on the right is The Old House at Home inn. Richard Wood held the licence in 1891.

West Street, c. 1900. The Star inn is now half tiled in grey slate. The large building on the left housed the Public Hall, a cinema and the fire station. It was also the headquarters of the Surrey Library Services until it was divided into five groups recently. The masons' yard and builders' yard are to the extreme right.

Further east along West Street, c. 1890. The King's Arms opened in around 1590 by Edward Goodwyn on the main road to Guildford and London and was designed to catch the travelling trade.

West Street looking east, 1972. The King's Arms has a new sign, and the Emporium is on the right. Just beyond the shop with the awning (58-61) is where William Mullins lived before he departed for Southampton, to join the *Mayflower* for Plymouth, Massachusetts. It is said to be the only surviving home of a Pilgrim Father in Great Britain. The railing on the left next to the car is the entrance to the United Reformed church. The Bell Inn, once called The Star, is a few doors up. There was yet another public house in this street: the Rose & Crown was on the south side of the street. It looks very much the same as it did a hundred years ago.

An advertisement for the West Street Pharmacy.

The Falkland Arms, which stands in Falkland Road, *c.* 1900. Miss Elizabeth Cotton, daughter of Sir Arthur Cotton, shared her father's enthusiasm for temperance and held religious meetings in a building known as the Beckenham Rooms in Falkland Road. Sir Arthur was noted for his jaunts around the town on his tricycle. He was a great engineer and was renowned for supplying water to the dry lands of India. He was nicknamed 'Irrigation Cotton'.

The exterior of the Falkland Arms, *c.* 1900. There used to be an iron horse trough to provide fresh water for the coach horses. Just around the corner in Hampstead Road is the Prince of Wales, another public house. There is yet another in Horsham Road called the Bush, five minutes' walk from the Prince of Wales. A third pub in the area, the Arundel Arms, closed its doors in the early 1990s.

Five

Social Events

The end of the High Street on Peace Day, 19 July 1919. The procession is led by the fire brigade and includes two nurses in uniform. Dunn's furriers shop is on the extreme left.

Election day, *c.* 1910. The election results were always announced on the steps of the Red Lion Hotel. One of the many butchers in Dorking stands to the right in his butcher's apron.

Outside the White Horse Hotel on Hunt Day, *c.* 1925. There is quite a crowd gathering and the hounds look ready for the off. The hotel now has garaging as well as stables.

Dorking's British School May Day celebrations, 1910. There was a school in Dorking as early as 1816. It is now called Powell Corderoy School. The school was formed by Mr T.E. Powell and Miss E.M. Corderoy. They are both buried in the Reigate Road cemetery, side by side.

The Dorking British School celebrations on Coronation Day, 1911. The children are dressed in all their finery with the boys in their sailor suits. Britannia stands high on the float holding her flag.

Coronation celebrations, 1911. Many people line the road waving their flags. There is quite a high ranking officer in the carriage.

The town band marching down the middle of the High Street on Coronation Day, 1911. The band was quite a prominent feature on such occasions.

Football in the Dorking streets. This is one of the last appearances of Taffer Boult's band, with leader Phil Stedman, on Shrove Tuesday 1895. The standard upon which the three painted footballs were taken in procession still exists and the inscription on the crossbar is 'Wind and water is Dorking's glory'. A collector with a tin box accompanied the band and invited contributions to meet the cost of repairing broken windows etc. Most of the shopkeepers erected barricades to protect their property and the damage, if any, was trifling. Any surplus was given to the bandsmen for beer.

Dorking Band performs at the Bandstand on a Saturday evening, c. 1922. The band was a big feature around the town at the turn of the century. They were well supported by the local traders. Their instruments were kept in the back room at the Surrey Yeoman.

The Local Defence Volunteers (Home Guard). Their headquarters were at the Salvation Army Hall. Only a few have been identified. Front row, second and third from left: William (Billy) John Edwards, Jack Burrell. Middle row, from left to right: ? Jorden, Bert Upfold, -?-, -?-, ? Spratley (with glasses). Fourth row, extreme right: Robert William Carpenter. Back row, from left to right: Freddy Stone, -?-, Charles Ackman. Also named but not identified are Walter (Wally) Kirby Sawyer and Mr Copus. There were other troops; 'P' Zone HQ was at Polesden Lacy and their Colonel in Chief was Lt Col. H.A. Pollock.

On parade again. The second soldier from the left is Robert Carpenter.

Marching through Dorking High Street towards the junction of West and South Streets, probably during Wings for Victory Week in 1943.

A Victory parade making its way past the White Horse Hotel, May 1945. The Guides, Cubs and Brownies form the end of the procession in the High Street.

The Local Defence Volunteers, or Home Guard as they were known, march through the High Street in full uniform, May 1945.

A Victory celebration parade outside Woolworths, May 1945. The nurses are in full uniform.

Waiting for the parade to pass on South Street, May 1945.

The celebration on VJ Night in 1945. The Bandstand in South Street is lit up for the occasion, and the band plays on. The golden cock that sits on top of the bandstand is now in Dorking Museum.

The Olympic Torch being carried through Dorking at 8 a.m. in 1948. Everybody was keen to see the torch. The smoke can just be seen in front of the car next to Woolworths. The Woolworths store name has changed over the years – it is no longer the '3d and 6d store'.

Six
The Outskirts

St Martin's spire is a prominent landmark from all Dorking's outskirts and outlying areas.

An aerial view of Vincent Lane and the southern end of the town, *c.* 1930. The terraced houses in Vincent Lane have not yet been built. St Margaret's House is on the corner, showing its walled garden; it is a car showroom now. Just beyond the walled garden is Powell Corderoy School, now St Joseph's Catholic School. The spire of the Wesleyan church in South Street is in the centre. The white building to the left is F.W. Mays' garage.

Looking towards the town from the Old Town station, *c.* 1907.

The view towards Ranmore from the top of Heath Hill at Cotmandene, *c.* 1930.

Looking east from the corner of Reigate Road and London Road, *c.* 1890. Pippbrook House is just visible behind the trees.

The old blacksmith's shop at the corner of the High Street, London Road and Reigate Road, *c.* 1890.

The blacksmith's shop again, *c.* 1900. The wooden building on the extreme left was at one time Israel Walker's cabinet workshop. The site is now a car park for council workers.

A traffic policeman stands guard to direct the cars at the junction of High Street, London Road and Reigate Road in the late 1920s. The sign post states that London is twenty-three miles distant.

The Embassy cinema, 1972. It started life as the Gaumont. Designed by Harry Weston, it opened its doors in 1938 as one of the largest and most modern of its time in the area. It could accommodate 1,290 people. It showed the most up-to-date films with first feature viewing Monday to Wednesday, changing for Thursday to Saturday. On Sunday there would be 'second-time-arounds', a chance to see the ones that you had missed the first time around. It closed as a cinema in 1973. It became a meeting hall for the Jehovah's Witnesses until it was demolished in 1983 to make way for a car park.

The Parade, 1972. These elegant timber-framed shops stand on the corner of the High Street and London Road. The Dorking branch of the TSB had its first premises here. Geoffrey Gifford was a well-known London ladies' hairdresser and the Dorking Hardware shop was popular. The first pet shop and the first laundrette in Dorking opened in this part of town. The Dorking Halls stand on the opposite side of the road.

Pixham Road, with Box Hill in the background, *c.* 1975. To the left is Bridge Motors, named after the bridge over the east-west railway line just beyond. The post office and shops here stopped trading in the mid 1990s. Edwin Lutyens' church is on the corner of Lesley Road.

The site of Dunn's furriers, *c.* 1910.

The Reigate Road cemetery was consecrated on 21 November 1855 and opened that month. The first burial (of Elizabeth Rose, a non-conformist) took place two days later. The first Church of England burial was that of Charles Wentworth, aged fifteen months. There are many notables buried in the cemetery, all of whom once lived in Dorking. They include Sir Arthur Cotton, the notable irrigation engineer, Miss Edith Powell and Mr T.E. Corderoy. There are also several members of the Bentall family. The poet George Meredith lies just inside the gates with many members of his family. Lastly, William (Bill) Brunel, a photographer who was noted for his fine pictures of motor cars and motor car racing, lies buried here. The cemetery is seen here in around 1895.

The Watermill, c. 1955. Just a quarter of a mile from the cemetery stands this timber-framed building which was for many years a hotel, with the only public swimming pool in Dorking. It has always had a fine restaurant with a loft bar. It was a watering hole for many motor-car enthusiasts and the local jazz club now meets there every week.

The Star and Garter hotel at the entrance of Station Road, in full splendour with flowers and shrubs adorning its entrance, *c.* 1890. It has always been a thriving hotel with a fine restaurant.

The Punch Bowl Inn, *c.* 1880. This public house stood directly opposite the Reigate Road Cemetery. It was built in 1780 on the edge of the Deepdene estate and has always been well known for its beer-garden. The area was the site of the Punch Bowl Fairs. Charles Rose comments in *Recollections of Old Dorking*: 'They [the fairs] were frequented by the younger members of the town. Early in the afternoon of Easter Monday, the road was thronged with groups making there way to the Fair.' The publican named in the 1891 census is James Greaves. The inn was redeveloped in 1971 and an annex of twenty-nine bedrooms were built. It became a motel and is now a Little Chef Burgerhouse and Happy Eater restaurant, and the name 'Punch Bowl' has been lost.

An aerial view of the town from the Nower, *c.* 1930. Sondes Place Farm is in the foreground but the new Sondes Place School is not yet built. Once again, St Martin's spire dominates the scene.

The Nower, *c.* 1921. This open land was once owned by the Barclay family of Bury Hill. On the celebration of Queen Victoria's Jubilee, access was allowed to the public.

Seven
Dorking's Large Estates

Deepdene Avenue in around 1920. There are no trees left on the avenue today, which is now the busy A24 which takes the traffic across the A25, past Box Hill and Mickleham and towards Leatherhead and London. The A24 was created during the early 1930s.

Gardeners posing for the camera, *c.* 1910. The large houses employed a large number of gardeners and other grounds staff in the early years of the century.

Deepdene House, a magnificent mansion owned by the Hope family, *c.* 1920. Thomas Hope was the eldest son of John Hope, a rich Amsterdam merchant. Thomas settled in England in 1796, and was a collector of vases, sculptures, pictures and works of art. Among his collection was the Hope Diamond. The house contents were sold at auction by Christie's in 1894. Thomas was also an author of fine books. The house was taken over by the railway and fell into disrepair. It was sadly demolished in the spring of 1969, although it had become a Grade III listed building. Now both house and grounds have disappeared.

The Denbies, c. 1910. The Denbies was once a vast estate of 3,900 acres, purchased from Thomas Cubitt by Lord Londborough in 1850, who was the grandson of William Denison, another successful builder. Cubitt hoped to rival Deepdene in size and splendour. The new house, built on the site of the old eighteenth-century one, contained over 100 rooms. It was a huge brick building with Italianate stucco details and similar in style to the east wing of Queen Victoria's Osborne House on the Isle of Wight, which Cubitt had built. Prince Albert was invited to Denbies at its completion, but Cubitt died in December 1855. His son George inherited the estate and continued his father's improvements. The estate eventually gave employment to 400 people. Denbies was demolished in 1953.

Denbies Lodge, the entrance to the estate.

Pippbrook House, now the local library. The earliest known owners of the house were the Atte Pyppe family in 1378. The first known house on the site was built in the 1750s by William Page. There is evidence of his living there from 1759-1764 and there is a painting hanging in the committee room at Lord's Cricket Ground which shows an elegant Georgian house with three storeys, set in fine gardens in the shadow of Box Hill. In 1817, William Crawford, MP for the City of London, acquired the property. On his death the house passed to his son, R.W. Crawford, who succeeded his father in every way and occupied the old mansion. Later, Sir Gilbert Scott transformed the mansion for the new owner, William Forman, adding a billiard room, library and porch to the existing Georgian house in 1855. He also replaced the old stone fireplaces with new marble ones, all carved with the Forman crest. Scott later added a museum with decorations and painted ceiling. The doors are ornately carved with leaves and trees of England. The ceilings are most beautifully painted and decorated in blues, reds, greens and yellows. The coat of arms of the Forman family can be seen at the entrance to the second floor. The stairway is wide, with a curved balustrade.

The front page of the *Daily Mirror* on 3 December 1931, recording the opening of the new Dorking Urban District Council offices by Lord Ashcombe.

The railway arrived in Dorking in 1849. The first line to open was the east-west, under the auspices of the Reading, Guildford & Reigate Railway Company, which ran a service from Redhill to Guildford. The old Dorking Town station (now known as Dorking West) included a goods yard. The station on the east side of the town (now known as Deepdene) was first called Boxhill and opened in 1851. When the new Denbies Wine Estate opened its doors to visitors, a light railway was installed to conduct visitors on a guided tour of the vines and vats.

Eight

Box Hill and Burford Bridge

His furrow oft the stubborn glebe has broke.

A view of the south face of Box Hill near the junction of Brockham Lane (now on the A25), *c.* 1900. Reigate Hill is in the distance. In Jane Austen's *Emma*, published in 1816, Emma Woodhouse chooses Box Hill for a picnic with friends. Later Jane Austen wrote 'Even Emma grew tired at last of the flattery and merriment, and wished herself walking quietly about with any of the others, or sitting almost alone and quite unattended to, in tranquil observation of the beautiful views beneath her.'

An aerial view of Dorking, *c.* 1940. The east-west railway line is clearly visible across the top of the picture. The A24 runs north to south, snaking past Deepdene House on the right and Cotmandene to the left. The roundabout is at the junction with the A25, going from east to west and passing through the town. The Fairfield and Parkway estates can be seen either side of the Meadowbank Recreation Ground.

Beneath the slopes of Box Hill stands the old coaching inn, the Burford Bridge Hotel, seen here in around 1890. The land on which it stands was once the property of Walter de Merton, the founder of Merton College at Oxford. It is thought that the first building on the site was built in 1629 and known as Cockscroft, which had a barn and orchards. In 1792 James Charman owned the property which had been renamed the Fox and Hounds. William Charman, son of James, developed the property into a substantial coaching inn. Lord Nelson, when visiting the inn, once gave the landlord two wicker table mats as a memento of the visit. The Charmans took the mementoes with them when they left Dorking.

Boxhill, Dorking.

By 1822 the Burford Bridge Hotel at the bottom of the hill was called the Hare and Hounds and was described as a favourite resort of bon-viveurs, and was said to be a regular stopping place for the fashionable Londoners who visited the neighbouring countryside. It later became known as the Burford Bridge Hotel. When it was put up for sale on 23 April 1856 it was described in the catalogue as 'The Hare and Hounds inn, better known ... and deservedly appreciated as The Burford Bridge Hotel ... in the Manor of Thorncroft ... for upwards of 60 years.'

Lord Horatio Nelson spent several days here with Sir William and Lady Hamilton in 1801, and wrote in his diary 'What a pretty place, and we were all very happy'. Later, Nelson and Lady Hamilton visited the Burford Bridge Hotel, and it is said that he courted her here; there is now a room named after her. It is also said that Nelson made a detour to see his fair lady here en route to Trafalgar, although this romantic tale is probably a myth. It is recorded that Nelson did spend several days at the hotel prior to the battle.

A map of the area around Dorking, 1920.

The Ford, the lowest part of the River Mole, *c.* 1860. The gap between Box Hill and Ranmore is known as the Dorking Gap. The railway should have run through the gap, but instead it passes through a tunnel beside the A24. The pass was used by the Romans as an easy way through the North Downs to the coast.

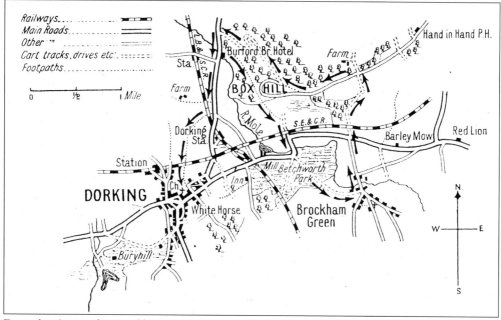

From the *Geographia Ramblers' Guide* No. 1, published in 1920: 'Though this is a comparatively short walk in miles, it involves two ascents of Box Hill, so that it entails as much as, if not more, exertion than some of the longer rambles.... The motor bus (107A) stops here [the Burford Bridge Hotel] on its journey from Clapham Common to Dorking. Beyond the inn, left as you face it, is a swing-gate opening up a steep uphill path.'

The road from Leatherhead to Dorking, leading from Mickleham to the entrance of the Zigzag and the Burford Bridge Hotel, *c*. 1900.

Pixholm (Pixham) Mill and Box Hill at a wide and fast-flowing point on the River Mole, *c*. 1900. Its proprietor then was James Dewdney, but the mill closed in 1910.

Box Hill Bridge, just below Box Hill Farm, c. 1900. Just yards away is the busy A25. The Dutch born painter, Abraham Hulk, lived for some time in Dorking and painted many of the local views. One hangs today in Pippbrook House.

Polesden Lacy, seen here around 1920, is an old estate created in 1203 for William de Polesden. It lies between Mickleham and Bookham. The estate was granted to John Norbury in 1470 by Thomas Slyfield. By 1784, the manor and house was known as High Polesden; Lacy was added during the eighteenth century. The old manor house was owned by Richard Brinsley Sheridan, the novelist. The present house was built by Thomas Cubitt in the early 1820s. The Hon. Capt. Ronald Grevill bought the property in 1906 and Edward VII became a frequent visitor. Mrs Grevill left the estate to the nation on her death in 1942. It is now part of the National Trust.

The Tithe Barn at the rear of the hotel, *c.* 1935. This dates from around 1600. It was transported from Abinger in the 1930s and re-erected on its current site. At about this time, a bathing pool of green culumax and marble was opened. To celebrate this the Australian women's breast-stroke team, then world champions, gave a swimming display.

The Burford Bridge, which spans the river near the hotel, *c.* 1900. Although it is a wide river at this point, it disappears beneath the chalk into the swallow holes. This disappearance caused much speculation over the centuries and gave rise to many legends and tales in folklore. William Camden wrote in *Britannia* (1610) that the river disappeared beneath the White Hill (as it was then known), only to rise again by Leatherhead Bridge.

The Slopes, Boxhill, Dorking.

'The Struggle', *c*. 1890. People flocked here in their hundreds to 'walk the struggle' and admire the spectacular view of three counties on a clear day. It is still a popular place, winter and summer. On Sunday mornings hundreds of motorcycle enthusiasts flock to the foot of the hill to show off their latest purchase, be it a Harley-Davidson, Triumph or Honda. Box Hill is now part of the National Trust and is a striking example of what was achieved purely by voluntary effort. This was the first gift to the Trust, and classed as 'the jewel in the crown'.

Zig Zag, Boxhill.

The Zigzag, seen here in 1938, was popular during the 'Golden Age of Motoring'. Many a car was tested along the winding road that leads to the top of the hill. Even before the motor car was invented, many walked this lane to gain inspiration, peace and tranquillity. Robert Louis Stevenson visited the hill and stayed at the Burford Bridge Hotel and wrote some of the *New Arabian Nights* while on one of his visits. Robert Bloomfield wrote of it: 'Where the Mole still silent glides, dwells peace and peace is wealth to me.' Even earlier, Samuel Pepys came from London to visit his friend and fellow diarist John Evelyn at Wotton. The hill can clearly be seen from Wotton church.

An engraving of the town from the road to the Denbies, *c.* 1880. The area has an air of peace and tranquillity that caused all who visited to fall in love with it. The white house to the far left of the frame is Deepdene. St Paul's church spire can be seen on the right of the skyline. The railway line and goods yard is seen in the dip of the valley.

Flint Cottage, the home of George Meredith, the novelist, *c.* 1890. Meredith lived in Flint Cottage for over forty years. Frequent visitors to Flint Cottage were J.M. Barrie, R.L. Stevenson and Henry James. Meredith wrote in 1882: 'Nowhere in England is richer foliage, or wilder downs and fresher woodlands'. Meredith named Juniper Bottom 'Happy Valley' and instigated the 'Sunday Tramps'. Among his followers were Leslie Stephen, James C. Robertson, Carlyle, R.L. Stevenson, and Hilaire Belloc. As he became gradually crippled, he insisted on continuing his jaunts by means of a bath chair, and was taken out each day to view his beloved Box Hill.

The chalk path along the top of the hill in around 1900. The path leads down to The Struggle, with a spectacular view of the Downs. There have been many visitors to Box Hill who have been able to say: 'The Hill gave me the inspiration that was needed.' John Keats walked the hill for inspiration and had joy in finishing one of his poems.

The Box Hill Fort in around 1900, testimony to a war never fought. It was built in the late nineteenth century at the instigation of General Sir E. Hamley. He started his campaign to build the fort during the time when the British Navy felt weak, and no longer competent to stem a French and Russian invasion due to their increasing strength. Hamley's idea was to enlist volunteers who would man forts positioned around London. His idea was approved by the Government in 1888, and the fort on the hill was built on a five-acre site.

The Swiss Cottage at Box Hill, c. 1900. The Hill was a playground for the exuberant Georgians, the adventurous Victorians and the playful Edwardians. During the warm days of spring and summer, hundreds of visitors would be seen climbing the slopes, walking, hiking, playing and soaking up the sun on the south and west sides of the hill, and resting for tea at the Swiss Cottage.

Looking towards Dorking from the eastern slopes of the hill, with Box Hill Bridge and the River Mole winding its way around the hill, c. 1860. The summit was given by Mr Leopold Salomons of Norbury Park as a memorial to George Meredith in 1914. Lodge Hill and later Juniper Bottom were donated by Miss A.M. Warburg in 1921. In 1923 a public appeal sponsored by *Country Life* magazine in 1935 allowed land around the Burford Lodge to be purchased. In 1939 Lord Beaverbrook donated land on Mickleham Downs adjoining White Hill. The estate now boasts 900 acres owned by the National Trust and another 300 acres under protection.

Dorking from the Memorial, Boxhill

There are many famous people who have been connected with Dorking and Box Hill. One notable gentleman was Major Peter Labelliere, a resident of the town. A memorial stone was erected and inscribed: 'An eccentric resident of Dorking was buried here head downwards 11 July 1800'. He was buried this way at his own request. He believed that when the world ended it would turn upside down, and if he was buried this way, he would be the right way up. There is rumour that his body was later removed and buried elsewhere. This view from the memorial dates from around 1935.

From *Country Walks* no. 3 by London Transport, published in 1937 at a cost of threepence. 'Box Hill needs no introduction. The new stepping-stones approach is worth trying – by those strong enough in limb and wind. On crossing the Mole – the pilgrims are said to have crossed here – it is preferable to ascend by the left-hand path.... For those who desire only to visit Box Hill for the view and pleasant loitering, without overtaxing their legs or respiratory organs, an easy ascent can be made by following the carriage-road, which is a little to the left of Burford Bridge as one faces the inn – an easy ascent through woods to the crest near the Fort Tea Gardens. On the left is Flint Villa, where George Meredith lived.'

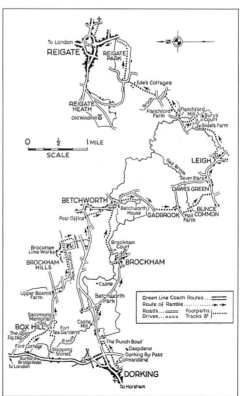

Box Hill Farm in 1890, owned by the Alexanders for many years. The tea room at the farm was just at the foot of the hill adjacent to the Old Reigate Road. Coach excursions and bicycle tours from London became very popular. One of the enterprising publicans of Dorking decided to make a profit from the captive visitors to Box Hill. He set up a small bar to give liquid refreshment to the visiting ladies and gentlemen, who would work up a thirst climbing the chalky slopes. This was soon to come to an end when a puritan element of the town decided to put a stop to the illicit sale of alcohol. One evening, a party of religiously minded men marched onto Box Hill and completely wrecked the bar, and poured its contents down the hill.

Donkeys on Box Hill, *c.* 1890. The donkeys were provided by Box Hill Farm for the pleasure of the visitors Other attractions for visitors included a tea room at the top of the Zigzag road and until the late 1960s there was a swimming pool.

The Keepers Cottage on top of the hill, *c.* 1909. Box Hill is named after the box trees which grow on the hill. The wood of the box is unusual: it is heavy and will not float and its density means that it was much sought after as a strong building material.

THE KEEPERS COTTAGE, BOX HILL.

The Lookout at the summit of Box Hill, *c.* 1946. It is due to the great generosity of Leopold Salomons of Norbury Park that the public now has the privilege of using the hill. To save the area for the nation, Salomons bought the land to save it from urban developers, and presented it to the people of England. It is undoubtedly one of the best known and most popular hills on the North Downs. The views from the summit are spectacular. Southwards are the South Downs, with Brockham, Betchworth, and Leigh closer by and, to the left, Reigate. Clearly visible on the horizon is the small village of Newdigate. The River Mole can bee seen running through Betchworth Park and can be easily traced on its journey towards Dorking. Looking towards the south-west is the prominent landmark of Leith Hill Tower.

The view from the summit towards Ranmore Common, Boxhill.

Ranmore Common from the summit of Box Hill, *c.* 1920. Windsor Castle can be seen on a clear day from the summit, as well as St Paul's and Westminster Abbey. The view of Box Hill and the surrounding valley of the Wealden fields is remarkable. Ranmore Common has been untouched over the centuries and the nineteenth-century church built by the first Lord Ashcombe is a particularly pretty sight.

A late eighteenth-century engraving by T. Allom of the view over Norbury Park, showing the gap in the hills. The Dorking Gap was made famous by a nineteenth-century military commander, Col. George Chesney, in an article in *Blackwoods Magazine* in May 1871. He informed the Government of his fear of a French invasion. It was an easy march to London. Chesney wrote a book entitled *The Battle of Dorking*. It has had many editions and told of the battle that could be fought if there was an invasion. It was immortalized by Sir Arthur Conan Doyle in one of his Sherlock Holmes novels.

Dorking town from the Box Hill Fort, *c.* 1950.

Box Hill is one of Southern England's most precious natural resources and loved by all who visit its chalky slopes. In the eighteenth and nineteenth centuries, hundreds of city folks would travel to Box Hill and Mickleham station to enjoy the country air, peace and tranquillity. It was also a well known haunt of the well-heeled city dwellers from London, who would abandon their shoes to spend a carefree day on the slopes.

Looking at Box Hill from the west in around 1920, showing the density of the woodland. Box, willow and elm can be seen, with the Ayrshire cows standing in a plush meadow sprinkled with buttercups. The view below is from the west with the covered hayricks on the farm by the side of the farm track. Box Hill is one of the most photographed places in Surrey. It has also been a film makers' paradise. Many a scene from a television drama or film can be recognized as being shot on Box Hill. The film crew of *The Saint* series were often seen here, and also those making Agatha Christie dramas. It has also often been a good backdrop for advertising purposes.

The views from Box Hill are perhaps one of the best known in the county. The height of the hill gives unbroken views of the Downs and Wealden Valley. The most famous part of the hill, which rises 400 sheer feet from the River Mole to the summit, has been noted as 'the grandest piece of natural river cliff in southern Britain'.

Box Hill in 1900, showing Pixham Mill. Another diarist fascinated by Box Hill was the formidable woman traveller, Celia Fiennes. Miss Fiennes lived in the late seventeenth and early eighteenth centuries and often travelled alone through England and Scotland, exploring the areas she visited. She wrote about her experiences, the countryside and its inhabitants. In the latter part of her life, she wrote about Box Hill, and how it was becoming a playground for the idle rich. She wrote: 'The greatest is Box Hill ... a vast vale of woods and enclosures.... There is a river that runs by a little town called Darken just at the foot of this hill, very famous for good trout and great store of fish; on this hill the top is covered with box, whence its name proceeds... There is other wood but it's all cut in long private walks – very shady and pleasant and this is a great diversion to the company.'

Birds Eye View of Dorking.

Box Hill could almost have been named because it is like a box in a theatre, affording surprisingly beautiful views, such as this 1890 panorama.

BOX HILL FROM THE DENBIES. — DORKING.

Box Hill from Denbies, *c.* 1890. As early as 1655, the area was being recommended in the diaries of John Evelyn and Samuel Pepys. Evelyn wrote: 'To see those rare natural bowers, cabinets and shady walks in the Box Copses ... here are such goodly walks and hills shaded with yew and box as render the place extremely agreeable, it seeming to be summer all winter for many miles prospect'.

High Ashurst, one of the fine houses near the top of Box Hill, *c.* 1890. The house is now no more. In 1923 a public appeal sponsored by *Country Life* led to the purchase of Ashurst Rough and White Hill in the Headley Valley. In 1926, local sponsorship and small gifts led to valuable land being protected. In 1935, as a result of a further national appeal also launched by *Country Life*, the land surrounding the Burford Lodge was purchased establishing it as protected land for the nation.

Looking towards Box Hill from the village of Brockham Green, *c.* 1910. John Keats (1795-1821) wrote after a long walk along the Mole: 'O thou would'st joy to live in such a place'. He was also a frequent visitor to Dorking and the hill; he came for inspiration, having found London 'dull'. He was eager to finish his poem 'Endymion'. On 22 November 1817, he wrote a letter home expressing his pleasure with the surroundings: 'There is a hill and dale, and a little river. I went up Box Hill this evening after the moonrise.... Came down again, and wrote some lines'.

Glory Woods, just south-west of the town centre, *c.* 1911. In 1927 Lord Francis Hope, afterwards Duke of Newcastle, presented the Glory Woods to the town of Dorking. They had once been part of the great estate of Deepdene.

Road widening is under way on Reigate Road, 1926. The view is towards the west, just before the Punch Bowl Inn and the cemetery.

Nine
Mickleham and Beyond

St Michael's church, Mickleham, *c.* 1920. Frances (Fanny) Burney married Monsieur d'Arblay here in 1793, calling it 'the little church with the squat tower'. George Meredith was also married here. Buried in the churchyard is Richard Bedford Bennet who became Viscount Bennet of Calgary. He was a Canadian barrister, became a politician and was Prime Minister of Canada in 1932. He retired to Juniper Hill in 1939.

Mickleham village, seen here around 1890, has had many prominent people in its midst, including George Meredith, Judge Gordon Clark, who wrote detective stories under the name of Cyril Hare, Dr Marie Stopes, Thomas Broadwood, David Evans, William Whiteley (founder of the London department store), W.H. Cullen of grocery store fame and Sir James Jeans the mathematician.

The Druids' Grove, Norbury Park, in 1930. It is said to be one of the loveliest estates in Surrey and has been preserved by Surrey County Council. Its most famous trees are the ancient yews: two of the biggest are over twenty-two feet round, and a path passes under one remarkable specimen, whose branches touch the ground. Some of the trees in this area bear strange names such as 'King of the Park', 'Horse and Rider', and the 'Fallen Giant'. It is said that the rare dotted chestnut moth can be seen at midnight in October, bloated with the juice of yew tree berries. During Meredith's time at Box Hill, he loved to send his visitors to see the yews.

The Fredley footpath at Mickleham, *c.* 1890.

Mickleham village street, a scene which would no doubt have been familiar to Fanny Burney who set up home here after her marriage to Monsieur d'Arblay, a fugitive from the French Revolution. Her most celebrated novels are *Evelina* and *Cecilia*. Fanny became the keeper of the Queen's robes for Queen Charlotte but retired after only five years with an annual pension of £100.

The Old Forge Café, *c.* 1937. This was a popular resting place for those looking for something less expensive than the Burford Bridge Hotel. Once the blacksmith's shop, it was turned into a café in the early years of the century and remained until the 1960s.

The bypass to Mickleham, now the A25, in 1936. The road was started during the Depression and attracted many workers from Wales and the north of England. Thanks to the bypass, Mickleham and Westhumble remain quiet villages.

Chalkpit Cottages beside the east side of the Mickleham bypass. Little has changed since, except for the disappearance of the oak trees. The turning to the Zigzag and Box Hill is a little way to the south (behind the camera) and the Old Forge Café is just out of view.

The Dorking to Leatherhead road at Mickleham, near the bottom of Box Hill. This picture dates from the 1880s, when the main road still passed through the village.

The west door of St Michael's church, Mickleham. The church and village were known to a number of famous eighteenth- and nineteenth-century characters, including Madame de Staël, the Marquis de Lafayette (who introduced the block system to New York's streets), Samuel Johnson and Charles Darwin.

Mickleham Church, West Door.

St Michael's church with its Norman tower. The *Victoria County History* states that the north tower and nave date from 1140. The chancel was added in the late twelfth century. The singing gallery was added in 1774 and an organ was acquired at the same time. By the beginning of the nineteenth century there was concern that the seating was insufficient for the parishioners; it then underwent repair.

The New National School, from an engraving by T. Allom, *c*. 1850. Bishop Wilberforce led the campaign to erect a school for the parish. He made an urgent appeal in 1830 and the money was provided by Sir George Talbot and others. The school opened in 1843 and the first headmaster was Caleb Howard, who retained the position for twenty-eight years.

Coldharbour Lane, 1895. Coldharbour is one of the highest villages in Surrey, lying 750ft up near the summit of Leith Hill, and has a fine view over the Weald. One of the main roads out of London used to pass through this tiny village before dropping steeply to the south.

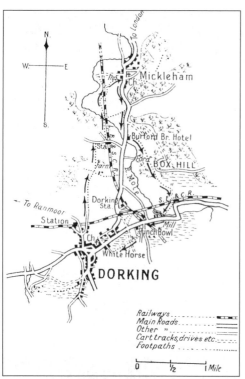

From the *Geographia Ramblers' Guide To Dorking* No.1, *c.* 1920. 'From the White Horse inn follow the road through the town forward and at the fork take the Guildford Road to Station Road on the right. Turn along this and take the right-hand fork just beyond the brook and keep on by it – a rough cart-track across the railway and alongside allotments. When clear of these, wide views open out, with Box Hill on the right as a dominating feature of the landscape. Hold to the track and where it forks follow the main right-hand branch down towards a farm.'

A woodland scene near Mickleham. The beauty and serenity of the countryside that surrounds the village have ensured that Box Hill and environs have developed as a Mecca for picnickers from London and elsewhere. As early as the seventeenth century, Daniel Defoe was shocked at the disgraceful behaviour of certain ladies and gentlemen, who would frolic through the woodland and consume much alcohol on a Sunday afternoon. The Running Horses and King William IV are, and were, convenient hostelries for the visitors.

The larch wood on Leith Hill in 1895. The trees were felled during the First World War, as larch has very tough, hard wood suitable for pit props, used in the trenches. Subsequent replantings ensure that larch continues to grow on the hill.

Dorking, Chart Lane.

Chart Lane, looking south, *c.* 1910. Dene Street begins at the junction of the High Street and changes its name to Chart Lane at the end of Cotmandene.

The edge of Dorking's valley. The area covering Box Hill, Dorking, the Holmwoods, Leith Hill, Ranmore and Coldharbour contains some of the finest woodland and natural habitats in Surrey. Generous donations of land and money by many public-spirited contributors over the years have helped to ensure that this hundred-year-old view varies little from today's prospect.